COOKING

THE

EAST AFRICAN

WAY

First published in the United Kingdom in 2010 by
Lerner Books,
Dalton House,
60 Windsor Avenue,
London SW19 2RR

Website address: www.lernerbooks.co.uk

This edition was updated and edited for UK publication by Discovery Books Ltd., First Floor, 2 College Street, Ludlow, Shropshire SY8 1AN

British Llibrary Cataloguing in Publication Data

Montgomery, Bertha Vining
Cooking the East African way. - New ed. - (Cooking around the world)
1. Cookery, African - Juvenile literature 2. Cookery - Africa, East - Juvenile literature
I. Title II. Nabwire, Constance R.
641.5'9676

ISBN-13: 978 0 7613 4394 3

Printed in China

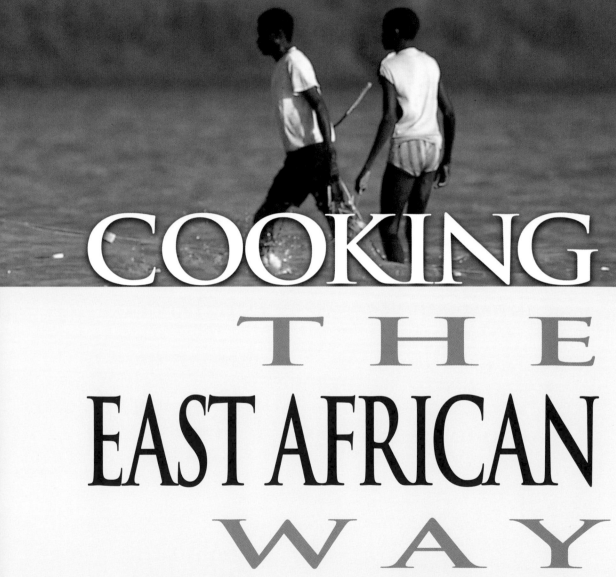

COOKING
THE
EAST AFRICAN
WAY

Bertha Vining Montgomery and Constance Nabwire

Lerner Books • London • New York • Minneapolis

Contents

Introduction

East Africa, home of grass savannahs (plains with few trees), elephants and safaris, is the Africa often featured in films and books. Most of the countries that make up East Africa – Ethiopia, Eritrea, Somalia, Kenya, Tanzania and Uganda – border the Red Sea, the Indian Ocean or Lake Victoria. Great Britain once controlled most of this part of Africa so, for a long time, British cuisine has been the food of choice. East Indian immigrants to the region introduced East Africans to Indian foods such as chapatis (Indian flat bread), pilau (a rice and meat dish), samosas (potato-stuffed pastries) and curry (a spicy meat and vegetable dish), which appear regularly on East African tables. Traditional East African cooking features meat stews flavoured with chillies.

People in Uganda and Kenya enjoy greens steamed with coconut milk, tomatoes and onions. (Recipe on page 41.)

AFRICA

EAST AFRICA

ERITREA

Red Sea

Asmara ★

Blue Nile River

Gulf of Aden

Addis Ababa ★

ETHIOPIA

River Shabeelle

SOMALIA

TEA

UGANDA

Kampala ★

Lake Victoria

KENYA

Nairobi ★

Mogadishu ★

Dar es Salaam ★

Lake Tanganyika

TANZANIA

INDIAN OCEAN

TEA

The Land and the People

The land of East Africa is varied, featuring soaring mountains and steep valleys, thick forests, barren deserts, lush coasts and fertile highlands. It contains the highest mountain in Africa – Mount Kilimanjaro – which is located in north-eastern Tanzania.

Lake Victoria, the second largest freshwater lake in the world, lies on the borders of Uganda, Kenya and Tanzania.

The equator runs through the countries of Kenya and Uganda, so it is not surprising that most of East Africa is hot all year-round. There are also highland areas that stay quite cool – often below 10°C – as well as mountains that are tall enough to be snowcapped. Rainfall is uneven across this part of Africa. Some areas have seasons of nearly constant rain, while others receive almost none at all. Drought has been a problem, especially in Ethiopia, where lack of rain has led to very serious food shortages.

Africans, Europeans, Middle Easterners and Asians all call East Africa home. Although most East Africans are black, they are divided into hundreds of ethnic groups, each with its own unique language and traditions.

The lives of East Africans vary greatly depending on whether they make their homes in the city or in the country. Those people who live in cities are more likely to have modern conveniences, such as electricity, ovens and televisions. East Africans who live in the country live very much as their ancestors did. They usually live in villages with relatives and other people of the same ethnic group. While some villages have houses made of modern materials such as cement and metal, many people still live in houses made of clay or dried mud with roofs of grass or palm leaves. In the majority of these villages, homes do not have running water or electricity.

Most East Africans who live in villages are farmers who work just outside the village on large plantations, growing crops such as coffee or tea. East African women spend their days caring for their children and gardening to feed the family. At harvest time, the women take any extra food to the village market. These open-air markets are places where people meet to talk with friends, buy fruit and vegetables and shop for cloth and other handmade goods.

Women also prepare the family meals. Most East African cooks don't have electricity or running water, so the traditional meals that they make take a lot of time. Women must gather firewood and carry water in buckets from a local well. Cooks use a traditional cooking tool called a pestle and mortar. A pestle is a club-shaped utensil that is used with a mortar (a sturdy bowl) to grind grain into flour or to pound foods, such as plantains. The women may also grind flour on a curved stone. Many East Africans, especially those who live in villages, still cook over an open fire in outdoor kitchens.

As food is sometimes scarce, East African cooks have learned to work with whatever they have. African dishes are versatile enough that if a certain ingredient is not available, it is always possible to substitute another or leave it out.

The Food

East Africans usually eat only two meals per day, one around lunchtime and the other in the evening. However, they also enjoy snacks, such as a piece of chapati, roasted or fried plantains or samosas. In the cities, these and other snack foods are sold on the street. It is unusual to eat something sweet for a snack, except perhaps for a piece of fruit or a doughnut.

Very few people have refrigerators, so the cooking of East Africa is based on fresh foods. In the villages, people grow all of their own fruit and vegetables in small gardens. Although the people who live in cities may have fridges and rely somewhat on tinned foods, they are still likely to visit the market every day to buy fresh fruit and vegetables.

Farmers grow wheat, rice, sweet potatoes, plantains and green vegetables such as spinach. In coastal and lakeside areas, fish is added to soups and stews. Meat and poultry are sometimes scarce. One reason that soups and stews are such staples in East Africa is that they can make a little meat stretch to feed many people. Many meals don't contain meat and chicken is usually saved for guests or special occasions. Meat, poultry and fish are usually served fresh, although they are sometimes preserved by smoking or drying.

For a long time, it was difficult to find books on East African cooking, because the recipes of British settlers were often featured instead. This may have been because most East African cooks do not follow written recipes when cooking. Recipes have traditionally been committed to memory and passed down through generations.

A woman in Tanzania uses rhythmic strokes to grind grain into a fine powder that will eventually be made into bread.

A market in Kenya displays pineapples, mangoes and citrus fruit, which thrive in the country's warmer areas.

The recipes in this book were collected from women from different countries all over East Africa and then adapted to western-measuring standards. A few of the recipes have been changed slightly to suit Western tastes. For the most part, however, the recipes are authentic. Once you have had a taste of East African cooking, you might try varying the meats and vegetables, making up your own combinations.

Festivals

Independence days and religious occasions give East Africans plenty of opportunities to celebrate throughout the year. On these special days, East Africans splurge on more expensive foods, such as lamb and other meats, to make meals something to remember.

Many East African countries, including Kenya and Somalia, were once British colonies. Each year these countries host a big party, featuring parades and special meals, to celebrate their independence. Kenya gained its independence on 12 December 1963. Each year, Kenyans travel to their home village to celebrate the day with family and friends. In big cities like Nairobi and Mombasa, parades wind down the streets. Traditional dancers and musicians dress in elaborate costumes and entertain the crowd. Since 1960, Somalians have celebrated Harnemo (Independence Day) on 26 June. Everyone has the day off from work and school. They dress in colourful clothes, wear gold jewellery and dance the day away. Foods such as rice, beef, camel, goat, fish and *halwud*, a dessert made with ginger and sugar, make Harnemo a day to look forward to.

Religious festivals occur throughout the year in East Africa. In Somalia, where most of the population is Muslim, Islamic festivals such as Ramadan, Eid ul-Fitr and Molit are important. Ramadan is the holiest month in the Islamic calendar. It was during this time that Muhammad, the Islamic prophet, received his first messages from Allah, or God. Muslims honour Allah during the month of Ramadan by fasting (refusing to eat or drink) from dawn until sunset. After the sun goes down, families gather at home for a light meal before bed. The next morning, Muslims get up at around 3.00 or 4.00 AM to eat breakfast before sunrise. At 7.00 AM on the last calendar. Although Ethiopian children don't look forward to a visit from Santa Claus, they do decorate a Christmas tree and receive presents from friends and relatives. Ethiopians light candles and listen to Christmas music. Families dress in white cotton robes, handmade for the occasion and go to church. Christmas dinner features roast lamb, rice, vegetables and a special bread called *hebyasha*.

Maskal is another Christian festival celebrated in Ethiopia. Ethiopian Christians believe that in the fourth century AD, Queen Helena, Emperor Constantine's mother, travelled to Jerusalem in

Women in East African villages are in charge of most farming jobs. Here, two villagers in Tanzania work together to plant sweet potatoes.

search of the cross on which Jesus was crucified. She found the cross and lit a huge bonfire to ward off evil spirits. Ethiopians celebrate the Maskal festival with parades that feature marching bands and hundreds of people carrying blazing crosses. After dark, fireworks and bonfires light up the night. People dance, sing and feast on roasted lamb, spicy stews called *wats*, and *injera*, a flat bread.

More than half of Uganda's population is Christian, but those people who practise traditional religions often participate in Christian celebrations and vice versa. A Christian priest or minister will usually lead the people in prayer and then traditional performers will dance to communicate with the spirits and ancestors. Food is an important part of every festival. Fresh fish, caught from one of Uganda's many lakes, is especially popular. No matter what the occasion, East Africans of all backgrounds make the day special with their favourite foods.

Before You Begin

Cooking any dish, plain or complicated, is easier and more fun if you are familiar with its ingredients. East African cooking makes use of some ingredients that you may not know. You should also be familiar with the special terms that will be used in various recipes in this book. Therefore, *before* you start cooking any of the dishes in this book, study 'The Careful Cook' and the following 'dictionary' of special cooking utensils, terms and ingredients. Then read through each recipe you want to try from beginning to end. Shop for ingredients and organize the equipment that you will need. Once you have assembled everything, you can begin to cook.

Samosas (recipe on page 36), a staple of East Africa, can be filled with minced meat or vegetables.

The Careful Cook

Whenever you cook, there are certain safety rules you must always keep in mind. Even experienced cooks follow these rules when they are in the kitchen.

- Always wash your hands before handling food. Thoroughly wash raw vegetables and fruits to remove dirt and chemicals. Wash uncooked poultry, fish and meat under cold water.
- Use a chopping board when cutting up vegetables and fruit. Be sure to cut carefully.
- Long hair or loose clothing can easily catch fire if brought near the hobs of a cooker. If you have long hair, tie it back.
- Turn all pan handles towards the back of the cooker so that you will not catch your sleeves or jewellery on them. This is especially important when younger brothers and sisters are around. They could easily knock a pan off and get burned or scalded.
- Always use an oven glove to take pans out of the oven. Don't use a wet cloth on a hot pan because the steam it produces could scald you.
- Lift the lid of a steaming pan with the opening away from you so that you will not get scalded.
- If you get burned or scalded, hold the burn in a bowl of cold water. Cold water helps to take the heat out of the burn. For more serious burns seek medical help immediately.
- If fat or cooking oil catches fire, throw bicarbonate of soda or salt at the bottom of the flame to put it out. (Water will not put out an oil or fat fire.) Call for help, and try to turn all the cooker controls to 'off'.

Cooking Utensils

colander – A bowl with holes in the bottom and sides. It is used for draining liquid from a solid food.

pastry brush – A small brush with nylon bristles used for coating food with melted butter, oil or other liquids

rolling pin – A cylindrical tool used for rolling out dough

skewer – A thin metal or wooden rod used to hold small pieces of food for grilling

slotted spoon – A spoon with small holes in it. It is used to remove solid food from a liquid.

spatula – A flat, thin utensil, usually made from metal or wood, that is used to lift, toss, turn or scoop up food

tongs – A utensil shaped like tweezers or scissors with flat, blunt ends used to grasp food

Cooking Terms

brown – To cook food quickly over a high heat so that the surface turns an even brown colour

garnish – To decorate with small pieces of food such as parsley sprigs

knead – To work dough by pressing it with the palms, pushing it outwards, and then pressing it over on itself

sauté – To fry quickly over a high heat in oil or fat, stirring or turning the food to prevent burning

simmer – To cook over a low heat in liquid kept just below its boiling point. Bubbles may occasionally rise to the surface.

stir-fry – To cook food in a small amount of oil over a high heat, stirring constantly

Special Ingredients

aubergine – A vegetable with shiny purple-black skin and cream-coloured flesh

black-eyed beans – Small, brown beans with a large black spot (from which they get their name)

cardamom – A spice of the ginger family, used whole or ground, that has a rich aroma and gives food a sweet, cool taste

chilli – A small, hot, red or green pepper

cloves – Dried buds from a small evergreen tree. Cloves can be used whole or ground to flavour food

coconut milk – The white, milky liquid extracted from coconut flesh, used to give a coconut flavour to foods. It is available in tins at most supermarkets.

coriander – A herb used ground or fresh as a flavouring or garnish

cumin – The seeds of a herb used whole or ground to give food a pungent, slightly hot flavour

filo pastry – Thin sheets of dough that can be wrapped around a filling and fried

garlic – A bulb-forming herb whose distinctive flavour is used in many dishes. Each bulb can be broken up into sections called cloves. Most recipes use only one or two cloves. Before you chop up a clove of garlic, you will have to remove the papery covering that surrounds it.

ginger root – A knobby, light brown root used to flavour foods

mung bean – A bean often used in Asian cooking that is available in supermarkets, Asian grocery stores or specialist shops

paprika – Dried, ground, sweet red peppers used for their flavour and colour

peanut – A small, pale brown nut that can be eaten roasted or cooked or ground up in recipes.

plantain – A starchy fruit that looks like a banana and must be cooked before it is eaten

seasoned salt – A commercially prepared mixture of salt and other seasonings

spring greens – The leaves of a plant related to the cabbage

stock cubes – Small cubes that make stock when combined with hot water

thyme – A fragrant herb used fresh or dried to season food

turmeric – A yellow, aromatic spice made from the root of the turmeric plant

vermicelli – Pasta made in long, thin strands that are thinner than spaghetti

yeast – An ingredient used in cooking to make bread rise and cause liquid to ferment

Healthy and Low-Fat Cooking Tips

East African cooking relies on many vegetables and legumes and not on cream and butter, so many dishes are naturally low in fat. You can lower the fat content in many of these dishes even further by eliminating the meat from the recipes. Some of the recipes featured in this book do require deep-frying. If you are particularly concerned about cutting fat from your diet, consider baking these items instead.

There are many things you can do to prepare healthy, low-fat meals. Here are a few general tips for adapting the recipes in this book. Throughout the book, you'll also find specific suggestions for individual recipes – don't worry, they'll still taste delicious!

Many recipes call for butter or oil to sauté vegetables or other ingredients. Using olive oil or sunflower oil instead of butter lowers saturated fat immediately, but you can also reduce the amount of oil you use – often by half. Sprinkling a little salt on the vegetables brings out their natural juices, so less oil is needed. It's also a good idea to use a small, non-stick frying pan if you decide to use less oil than the recipe calls for. Using cooking sprays to grease cooking pans is also an option.

Another common substitute for butter is margarine. However, before making this substitution, consider the recipe. When desserts call for butter, it's often best to use butter, as margarine may noticeably change the taste or consistency of the food.

For some recipes, you might like to use a low-fat coconut milk in place of coconut milk to lower the fat content. This substitution works well in recipes for soups. When stock is called for, use low-fat and non-fat varieties to cut down the fat content of the dish.

There are many ways to prepare meals that are good for you and still taste great. As you become a more experienced cook, try experimenting with recipes and substitutions to find the methods that work best for you.

Colourful herbs, pulses and spices such as these, are used in a variety of different East African dishes.

An East African Table

Before eating, East Africans wash their hands in a bowl of soapy water placed near the table. Family and friends may dine at a table with chairs, but in small villages, people are just as likely to take a seat on the floor. A typical East African meal features a main dish — usually a thick soup or stew made with vegetables, meat, poultry or fish — served on individual plates. A starchy food (carbohydrate), such as chapati, is served on a communal plate. The diners break off a piece of chapati and use it to scoop up some of the food on their plate.

Although diners in restaurants may use cutlery, the traditional way to eat in East Africa is to use the right hand. Dinner time is a chance for people to relax, talk and catch up on the day's news. After a leisurely main course, East Africans might enjoy fruit such as mangoes or plantains for dessert.

Plantains are banana-like fruits that are hard and starchy, and must be cooked before eating. Plantains can be fried (front), boiled with vegetables (back left) or grilled (back right). (Recipes on pages 42-43.)

An East African Menu

East Africans traditionally eat two meals a day, one at noon and one in the evening. The two meals are basically the same. They are usually made up of a soup or stew served with some sort of starchy food, such as chapati or *matoke* (mashed plantains). Desserts are more common in the city than they are in rural villages. Below are two East African dinner menus.

DINNER #1

Chapatis

Samosas

Avocado and papaya salad

Peanut sauce with rice

Kashata

SHOPPING LIST:

Produce

5 spring onions
2 large avocados
1 small papaya
1 red grapefruit
1 small head of lettuce
1 medium onion
2 medium tomatoes
1 small aubergine

Dairy/Egg/Meat

700g of extra-lean minced lamb or 4 medium potatoes
150g of frozen peas

Tinned/Bottled/Boxed

vegetable oil
lemon juice
olive oil
1 bag of desiccated coconut or 225g of unsalted peanuts

Other Ingredients

salt
375g of wholemeal flour
cumin seed
garlic powder
seasoned salt
black pepper
1 packet of filo pastry
100g of smooth, sugar-free peanut butter
rice (100g per person)
130g of sugar
cinnamon

DINNER #2

Ethiopian flat bread

Greens with coconut milk

East African plantain soup

Fresh steamed fish

Vermicelli and raisins

SHOPPING LIST:

Produce

450g of spring greens (or spinach or kale)
3 medium onions
3 large tomatoes
6 medium tomatoes
2 or 3 green plantains
1 clove of garlic

Dairy/Egg/Meat

1kg fresh or frozen whole, filleted fish (red snapper, halibut or cod)

Tinned/Bottled/Boxed

45ml of soda water
225ml of coconut milk
1.4 litres of chicken or vegetable stock
vegetable oil
vermicelli pasta
35g of raisins
35g of chopped dates
30g of chopped walnuts

Other Ingredients

250g of self-raising flour
salt
pepper
cardamom – ground
45g of sugar

Staples and Snacks

Mild-flavoured staples, such as rice and bread, are natural accompaniments to East Africa's hearty soups, stews and sauces. These foods are often used as 'utensils' to scoop up other foods, and some, such as chapatis, can also be eaten alone as a snack.

East Africans eat many snacks. These snacks, which can also be served as appetizers, are usually very nutritious and actually amount to 'mini-meals'.

Rice pancakes (front) and chapatis (back) are popular snacks. The pancakes go well with jam, and the chapatis get an extra kick when sprinkled with a little sugar. (Recipes on pages 32-33.)

Chapatis (Kenya, Tanzania, Uganda)

In Africa, chapatis are considered a luxury, because only those who can afford to buy imported flour can make them.

½ tsp of salt

300g of wholemeal flour

175ml plus 1–3 tbs. vegetable oil

175–225ml of water

1. In a large bowl, combine the salt and 250g of flour. Add 175ml of oil and mix well. Add the water, little by little, stirring after each addition, until the dough is soft. Knead the dough in the bowl for 5 to 10 minutes.

2. Sprinkle about 25g of flour onto a flat surface. Take a 5 cm ball of dough and, with a floured rolling pin, roll out into a 3mm thick circle the size of a saucer. Repeat with the remaining dough, sprinkling the flat surface with the remaining flour if the dough sticks.

3. Heat 1 tbsp of oil in a large frying pan over a medium-high heat for 1 minute. Fry the chapati for 3 to 5 minutes per side or until it is brown.

4. Remove from the pan and drain on pieces of kitchen towel. Fry the remaining chapatis, adding more oil if necessary.

5. Serve immediately or cover until ready to serve.

Preparation time: 25 minutes
Makes 6 chapatis

Rice Pancakes (Kenya)

1 tbsp (approximately) of dry yeast

up to 225ml of warm water (40°C)

190g of sugar

420g of rice flour

¼ tsp of ground cardamom

50ml of coconut milk

vegetable oil

Yeast makes these pancakes light and airy. If the yeast does not start to foam after about 5 minutes in warm water, it is not working properly. Try again with new yeast.

1. In a small bowl, dissolve the yeast* in 120ml of warm water. Add a pinch of sugar and set it aside in a warm place for about 5 minutes or until the yeast mixture foams.

2. In a large bowl, combine the sugar, flour and cardamom. Add the coconut milk and the yeast mixture and stir. The mixture should have the consistency of pancake batter. If it is too thick, stir in water, little by little, until the batter runs slowly from the spoon.

3. Cover the bowl and set it in a warm place for about 1 hour, until the mixture nearly doubles in size.

4. Heat 1 tbsp of oil in a large frying pan over a medium-high heat. Pour a ladleful of the batter into the pan and spread it with a spoon to form a pancake about the size of a saucer. Cover the pan and cook the pancake for 1 to 2 minutes or until it turns golden brown on the bottom. Sprinkle the pancake with a few drops of oil and turn it over with a spatula. Cover and cook for another 1 to 2 minutes or until it is golden brown on the other side. Repeat with the remaining batter, adding more oil when necessary.

Preparation time: 2 hours
Makes about 10 pancakes

Meat on a Stick (Ethiopia, Uganda)

The seasoned meat and onions can also be cooked in a frying pan with a little vegetable oil. In East Africa, the skewered meat is cooked over hot coals.

1 tsp of cayenne pepper

1 tsp of garlic powder

½ tsp of seasoned salt

700g of beef tenderloin or rump steak, cut into bite-sized pieces

1 medium onion, peeled and cut into 2.5 cm pieces

1. Combine the pepper, garlic powder and seasoned salt in a wide, shallow bowl. Add the beef pieces and mix with your hands to coat the meat with the spices.

2. Preheat the grill.

3. Thread the beef and onion pieces onto eight 30-cm long skewers. Grill for 4 to 5 minutes on each side or until the meat is tender.

Preparation time: 20 minutes
Makes 8 skewers

Before grilling the meat in this appetizer, East African cooks cover it with a mixture of cayenne pepper, garlic powder and salt to give it extra flavour.

Samosas

This snack, which originated in India, is a favourite in East Africa. In the cities, samosas are sold on street stalls.

700g of extra-lean minced lamb*

½ tsp of cumin seed

5 spring onions, chopped

a pinch of garlic powder

a pinch of seasoned salt

a pinch of black pepper

25g of flour

2 tbsp of water (or one egg, beaten)

1 packet of filo pastry

200ml vegetable oil

1. In a large frying pan, break up the minced lamb* with a fork. Add the cumin, spring onion, garlic powder, seasoned salt and black pepper and mix well.

2. Brown the meat over a medium heat. Drain off the fat and set the meat aside.

3. In a small bowl, combine the flour and water (or the beaten egg) and stir to make a paste.

4. Carefully cut the filo pastry into 15 x 15cm squares.

5. In a large frying pan, heat the oil over a medium-high heat for 3 to 4 minutes. With tongs, carefully place a samosa into the oil. The samosa should fry until it is golden brown, for about 3 minutes. If it takes longer than this, increase the temperature of the oil. Remove the samosa from the oil with a slotted spoon and drain it on kitchen towel. Repeat the process with the remaining samosas, frying 3 or 4 at a time.

How to fill samosas:

1. With a pastry brush, brush all 4 edges of the pastry with the flour and water mixture.

2. Place about 1 tbsp of the meat mixture just above the centre of the pastry.

3. Fold the pastry in half over the filling to form a triangle and press the edges together to seal.

4. Repeat with the remaining pastry.

Preparation time: 1 hour
Makes about 24 samosas

* To make this a vegetarian dish, replace the minced lamb with potatoes and peas. Peel, cut and boil 4 medium-sized potatoes. When they are soft, drain and mash. Mix in 150g of peas and the spices. Fill the smaosas as instructed.

Fruits and Vegetables

Many varieties of fruit and vegetables grow in East Africa. They are an important part of East African cooking. What people don't grow in their own gardens, they buy in open-air markets that offer everything from bananas and cucumbers to guavas and yams. The fruit and vegetable dishes in this book can be eaten alone for a snack, as a light lunch or supper, or they can be served as side dishes.

Avocados, papayas and grapefruit liven up this fresh fruit salad (recipe on page 40). Open-air markets sell many different types of fruit that are grown throughout East Africa.

Avocado and Papaya Salad

This salad is popular in Kenya. Although salads were not served on East African tables until colonial times, they have become more common in modern times.

2 large avocados

1 small papaya

1 red grapefruit

1 small lettuce

1 tbsp of lemon juice

2 tbsp of olive oil

salt and pepper to taste

1. Slice the avocados in half and remove the stones. Slice the papaya in half and remove the seeds. Scoop out the fleshy pulp from both with a spoon.

2. Cut the fruit into 2.5 cm pieces and combine them in a bowl.

3. Peel the grapefruit and divide it into segments. Peel the pith (thin skin) from each segment.

4. Cut each segment in half and add them to the avocado and papaya mix.

5. Wash the lettuce and use kitchen towel to pat the leaves dry.

6. Arrange the lettuce leaves on a plate. Spoon the fruit mixture over the leaves.

7. In a small bowl, use a fork or whisk to combine the lemon juice, olive oil, salt and pepper.

8. Drizzle the dressing over the salad and serve.

Preparation time: 20 minutes
Serves 4 to 6

Greens with Coconut Milk (Kenya, Uganda)

175ml of water

450g of fresh spring greens,*
cleaned and chopped

1 medium onion, peeled and
chopped

3 large tomatoes, cubed

225ml of coconut milk

a pinch of salt

1. In a large saucepan, bring the water to the boil over a high heat. Add the greens, reduce the heat to low and simmer for 4 to 5 minutes.

2. Add the onions, tomatoes, coconut milk and salt and stir well. Cook, uncovered, for 20 more minutes. Serve hot.

Preparation time: 35 minutes
Serves 4 to 6

* Greens, such as spinach or kale, can
be substituted for the spring greens.

Versatile Plantains

Plantains are an important food in East Africa. Although it is a member of the banana family, the plantain is often served as a vegetable. For variety, try adding tomatoes, onions, fresh spinach or a dash of curry powder to boiled plantains.

Boiled Plantains

2 large, firm, green plantains*

a pinch of salt

butter, to taste

1. Wash and peel the plantains. Cut them into 2.5 cm pieces and place them into a large pan.

2. Cover the plantains with water and add the salt.

3. Bring to the boil over a high heat. Reduce the heat to medium-low, cover and simmer for 10 minutes or until the plantains can be easily pierced with a fork. Serve them hot with butter.

Preparation time: 10 to 15 minutes
Serves 4

* Green plantains are not yet fully ripe. They can withstand the boiling process better than yellow (ripe) plantains.

Fried Plantains

3 large, yellow plantains

vegetable oil

1. Wash and peel the plantains. Slice them into thin circles.

2. In a large frying pan, heat 5 mm depth of oil over a medium high heat for 4 to 5 minutes.

3. Add the plantain slices and fry them for 4 to 5 minutes or until they are golden brown on both sides.

4. Remove them from the oil with a slotted spoon and drain them on pieces of kitchen towel.

Preparation time: 10 to 15 minutes
Serves 4

Grilled Plantains

3 large, yellow plantains

1. Wash the plantains and cut them in half lengthways and widthways. Do not peel.

2. Preheat the grill.

3. Grill, skin side down, for 5 to 7 minutes or until the plantains can be easily pierced with a fork and aren't sticky.

4. When they are cool enough to handle, peel the plantains and serve.

Preparation time: 10 to 15 minutes
Serves 4

Sauces and Stews

East African sauces and soups are quite similar to each other. Soups are served with a starchy food, such as chapatis, on the side for dipping, while sauces, which are thicker than soups, are often served with rice. Stews are heartier than soups and sauces and usually make up the main part of the meal.

Peanut sauce (recipe page 48) uses peanut butter, which is protein-rich, as a main ingredient. It can be served instead of meat over rice, sweet potatoes or plantains.

Choroko Sauce (Uganda)

Although the flavour will be different, choroko sauce can also be made with split peas.

300g of dried mung beans

2 tbsp of vegetable oil

3 medium tomatoes, cut into
    bite-sized pieces

1 large onion, peeled and chopped

3 or 4 cloves of garlic, peeled and
    crushed

½ tsp of seasoned salt

a pinch of salt

a pinch of black pepper

120ml of water

1. Place the beans into a bowl and cover them with cold water. Leave them to soak overnight.

2. Drain the beans in a colander.

3. Fill a medium saucepan half full of water and bring it to the boil over a high heat. Add the beans and cook them for 1 to 1½ hours or until they are tender.

4. Drain the beans in a colander and place them into a medium bowl. Mash them well with a fork.

5. In a large frying pan, heat the oil over a medium heat for 1 minute.

6. Add the tomatoes, onions and garlic and sauté until the onions are transparent.

7. Add the mashed beans, seasoned salt, salt, black pepper and 120ml of water and simmer for 15 to 20 minutes. Serve over rice or with chapatis.

Soaking time: overnight
Preparation time: 2 hours
Serves 4 to 6

Peanut Sauce

This sauce is made from peanuts. Peanut sauce is often substituted for meat dishes, although it is also served with dried meat and dried fish.

2 tbsp of vegetable oil

I medium onion, peeled and chopped

2 medium tomatoes, cut into bite-sized pieces

I small aubergine, with or without peel, cut into bite-sized pieces

90g of smooth peanut butter*

60ml of water

rice to serve

1. In a large frying pan, heat the oil over a medium heat. Add the onions and sauté until they are transparent.

2. Add the tomatoes and cook for 5 minutes. Add the aubergine and cook for 5 more minutes.

3. In a small bowl, combine the peanut butter and the water and stir to make a paste. Add it to the tomato-aubergine mixture and stir well.

4. Reduce the heat to medium-low and simmer, uncovered, for 10 minutes or until the aubergine is tender.

5. Serve with rice, potatoes, sweet potatoes or plantains.

Preparation time: 30 minutes
Serves 4 to 6

* This recipe works best if it is made with natural peanut butter with no added sugar.

Banana and Meat Stew

500g of beef, cubed

500ml of water

2 onions, sliced

2 tomatoes, peeled* and sliced

2 tbsp of oil

2 medium green plantains, or 4 small green bananas, washed, peeled, sliced and placed in a bowl with cold water

225ml of coconut milk

salt and pepper, to taste

1. Place the meat and water into a pan and simmer them for 1 hour.

2. Sauté the onion and tomato in hot oil in a large frying pan until the onions are soft and golden.

3. Add the cooked meat, plantains or bananas and the coconut milk. If the coconut milk does not cover the meat, add some of the meat stock.

4. Season with salt and pepper. Simmer gently until the bananas are cooked and the meat is tender. If you are using regular bananas, only add them 15 to 20 minutes before the meat is done.

Preparation time: 1½ hours
Serves 4 to 6

* Tomatoes are easier to peel if they are first put in a bowl and covered with boiling water for 5 minutes.

Main Dishes

In East Africa, a thick, hearty stew is likely to be the main dish at nearly every meal. Such dishes feed more people at less cost and may often not contain any meat at all. On occasion, however, meat, vegetables and starchy foods, such as, plantains, rice or chapatis may be served separately. Meat-based dishes are not eaten daily, because meat is expensive.

Meat curry (recipe on page 53) can be made with chicken, lamb or goat.

Luku (Ethiopia)

Because of the high cost of chicken in East Africa, luku is usually reserved for special occasions.

8 hard-boiled eggs*

175ml of vegetable oil

750-900g of chopped onion

4.5 tbsp tomato puree

120ml of water

2 tsp of salt

¾ tsp of black pepper

1 tbsp of finely chopped garlic

2 tsp of paprika

¼ tsp of ground cumin (optional)

8 pieces of chicken, rinsed and
    patted dry with kitchen towel

1. Remove the shells from the hard-boiled eggs while they are still warm. With a sharp knife, make 4 or 5 shallow cuts on both sides of each egg. Set them aside.

2. In a large pan, heat 2 tbsp of oil over a medium-high heat for 1 minute. Add the onions and sauté them for 8 to 10 minutes or until the onions start to turn brown.

3. Reduce the heat to medium and add the tomato puree and water. Stir well. Cook for 10 minutes, then add the remaining oil. Cook for 5 more minutes.

4. Add the salt, black pepper, garlic, paprika, cumin and chicken. Reduce the heat to low and simmer, uncovered, for about 30 minutes.

5. Add the eggs, cover and cook for 10 minutes or until the chicken is tender.

Preparation time: 1 hour and 15 minutes
Serves 6

* To make hard-boiled eggs, place the eggs in a pan and cover them with cold water. Bring them to the boil and cook for 15 to 20 minutes.

Meat Curry

110ml of vegetable oil

75g plus 2 tbsp of chopped onion

4 cloves of garlic, peeled and finely
chopped

A 2.5-cm piece of ginger root,
peeled and chopped

2 tsp of cumin seed

4 whole cardamom pods

1 cinnamon stick

4 whole cloves

½ tsp of cayenne pepper

1 tsp of turmeric powder

160g of tomato puree

4 to 6 pieces of chicken, rinsed and
patted dry with kitchen towel

2 medium potatoes, peeled and
quartered

20g of fresh coriander

1. In a large frying pan, heat the oil
   over a medium heat for 1 minute.
   Add the onion, garlic, ginger root,
   cumin, cardamom, cinnamon stick,
   cloves, cayenne pepper and turmeric
   and stir.

2. Stir in the tomato puree and cook
   for about 10 minutes or until the
   tomato puree separates from the oil.
   Stir to blend the oil and the tomato
   puree.

3. Add the chicken, reduce the heat to
   low and cover. Simmer for about
   35 minutes.

4. Add the potatoes, cover and simmer
   for 15 minutes or until they are
   tender.

5. Add the coriander and simmer,
   uncovered, for 10 more minutes.

Preparation time: 1 hour and 15 minutes
Serves 4 to 6

Fresh Steamed Fish (Uganda)

In East Africa, this dish is made with a whole fish — with or without the head. This recipe works well with red snapper.

55ml of vegetable oil

2 medium onions, peeled and chopped

1 clove of garlic, peeled and chopped

3 medium tomatoes, chopped

½ tsp of salt

¼ tsp of black pepper

1kg of whole, filleted fish

1. In a large frying pan, heat the oil over a medium heat for 1 minute. Add the onions and sauté until they are transparent.

2. Add the garlic, tomatoes, salt and black pepper and mix well.

3. Place the fish in the centre of the tomato mixture. Cover and simmer for about 25 minutes or until the fish is tender and flaky.

Preparation time: 45 minutes
Serves 4 to 6

Tomatoes from the open-air market and freshly caught fish make this East African dish even more appetizing.

Vegetable Casserole (Uganda)

The variations of this colourful vegetable casserole are endless. Make it with the vegetables listed here or use your own favourites.

2 tbsp vegetable oil

I small onion, sliced and separated into rings

I medium aubergine, unpeeled, cut into bite-sized pieces

I small red pepper, cored and thinly sliced

I or 2 cloves of garlic, peeled and crushed

450g of fresh spinach, cleaned and chopped

I small courgette, peeled and sliced

2 medium tomatoes, cut into wedges

½ tsp of salt

¼ tsp of black pepper

1. In a large frying pan, heat the oil over a medium-high heat for 1 to 2 minutes.

2. Add the onions to the pan and stir-fry them for 2 to 3 minutes. Continue to add the vegetables to the pan in the order that they are listed, stir-frying each for 2 to 3 minutes before adding the next.

3. Stir in the salt and black pepper. Cover the pan, reduce the heat to low, and simmer for 10 to 15 minutes stirring occasionally, until the vegetables are tender.

4. Serve immediately.

Preparation time: 45 minutes
Serves 4 to 6

Pilau

For variety, you can add other vegetables, such as cabbage, carrots or green beans, to this popular rice dish originally from India.

2 tbsp of butter or oil

2 large onions, chopped

2 cloves of garlic, crushed

450g of lean lamb,* cut into 4 cm cubes

2 tomatoes, peeled and sliced

250ml water

475ml of coconut milk

225g of rice

½ tsp of cardamom seeds

1 stick of cinnamon

2 tsp of salt

1½ tsp of lemon juice

1 tsp of oil or melted butter

1. Heat 2 tbsp of butter or oil in a heavy frying pan.

2. Add the onions and garlic and sauté until they are golden.

3. Mix in the meat and tomatoes and cook, stirring constantly, until the meat begins to brown.

4. Add 250ml of water and simmer for 20 to 30 minutes.

5. Add the coconut milk, rice, spices and lemon juice and stir to combine. The water and coconut milk should cover the rice by 2.5 cm. If it doesn't, add more water.

6. Cover the pan and simmer until the rice is tender (about 20 to 25 minutes). Use a fork to stir.

7. Remove from the heat and sprinkle with 1 tsp of oil or melted butter.

8. Pre-heat the oven to 190°C. Place the pan in the oven for about 20 minutes, or until all the moisture is absorbed.

* To make this a vegetarian dish, leave out the meat and add any or all of the additional vegetables suggested above. You may also use chicken, fish or tofu instead of lamb.

Preparation time: 2 hours
Serves 4 to 6

Desserts

Desserts have not traditionally been part of the East African diet. While there is more interest in desserts than there used to be, an East African meal is still far more likely to be followed by a piece of fresh fruit, such as an orange or a mango, than any sort of cake or pie. The following desserts are typically East African, because none of them is too rich or too sweet.

Small strips of a pasta called vermicelli combine well with raisins, dates and walnuts in this simple dessert. (Recipe on page 60.)

Vermicelli and Raisins (Kenya)

2 tbsp of vegetable oil

250g of vermicelli, broken into 2.5 cm pieces

475ml of hot water

¾ tsp of ground cardamom

45g of sugar

35g of raisins*

35g of chopped dates (optional)

30g of chopped walnuts (optional)

1. In a large frying pan, heat the oil over a medium heat for 1 minute. Add the vermicelli and sauté until it is lightly browned.

2. Slowly add 475ml of hot water. Stir in the cardamom, sugar, raisins, dates and walnuts.

3. Cover, reduce the heat to medium low and simmer, stirring occasionally, for about 10 minutes or until all of the water is absorbed and the vermicelli is tender.

Preparation time: 20 minutes
Serves 4 to 6

*If you leave out the dates and nuts, increase the amount of raisins by 75g.

Kashata

These sweet treats are popular during festivals throughout East Africa.

130g of sugar

½ tsp of cinnamon

150g of grated or desiccated coconut or 225g of unsalted peanuts, finely chopped

1. In a heavy frying pan, heat the sugar until it melts (for about 10 to 15 minutes), stirring constantly. The melted sugar will be dark brown and syrupy.

2. Add the cinnamon and the coconut or peanuts.

3. Cook for about 2 minutes, or until the sugar turns light brown.

4. Remove from the heat and leave it to cool.

5. When the mixture is cool enough to handle, form 2.5 cm balls and place them on greaseproof paper until they are set.

Preparation time: 30 minutes (plus cooling time)
Makes about 20 balls

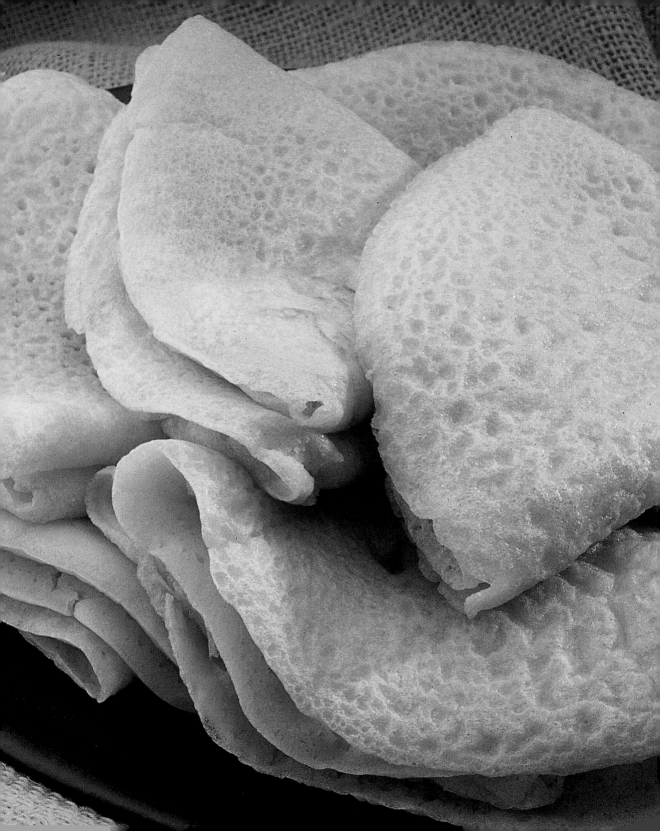

Festival Food

The diversity of East Africa's history adds variety to the area's festivals. All of the countries, except Ethiopia (which was never a colony), celebrate achieving independence from European colonial rule. Many festivals honour religious events. Islamic, Christian and traditional observances may prevail, depending on where the celebrations are taking place. No matter what the occasion, local cooks make the day special by preparing favourite foods.

In Ethiopia, injera is the traditional flat bread made from a local grain called teff. The recipe on page 64 uses self-raising flour.

Ethiopian Flat Bread/*Injera*

This bread, a staple throughout Ethiopia, is often eaten as part of the Maskal festival.

700ml of warm water

250g of self-raising flour

45ml of soda water

vegetable oil

1. Pour the warm water into a blender or food processor. Add the flour, cover and blend for 10 seconds. Turn the blender onto high and mix for 30 seconds, until smooth.

2. Pour the batter into a mixing bowl and add the soda water. Mix with a spoon. The batter should have the consistency of heavy cream.

3. Heat a 25-cm frying pan to a medium heat. Spread ½ tsp of oil over the pan with a pastry brush or paper towel. Pour a ladleful of the batter to one side of the pan. Quickly tilt the pan to spread the batter evenly over the bottom.

4. Small bubbles will soon appear on the surface and the edges of the pancake will curl away from the pan. After 1 minute, use a spatula to remove the injera. Place it onto a tea towel to cool. The finished injera should be white and easy to bend. Repeat the process until all of the batter is used up.

5. Fold each injera into quarters and stack them on a plate to serve.

Preparation time: 30 minutes
Serves 6 to 8

Rice with Fish/Wali na Samaki

Wali na samaki would be served for Eid ul-Fitr or Christmas.

2 green peppers, deseeded and chopped

1 onion, chopped

450g of chopped tinned tomatoes

475ml of water

the juice of one lemon

1 tsp of grated lemon rind

½ tsp of cayenne pepper, or to taste

3 bay leaves

salt and pepper to taste

1–1.3kg of skinless fish fillets such as red snapper, halibut or cod

100g of flour

vegetable oil

800g to 1kg of cooked rice

1. Combine the first nine ingredients in a large saucepan and stir. Bring to the boil over a high heat.

2. Cover with a tight-fitting lid and simmer the sauce for 30 minutes. Remove the bay leaves. Keep the sauce warm until you are ready to serve it.

3. Preheat the oven to 90°C. Wash the fish fillets in cold water.

4. Pour the flour onto a plate. Dip the fillets in to the flour, shaking off the excess. Place them on a clean plate.

5. Heat 2 tbsp of oil in a large frying pan over a medium-high heat. Add a few of the pieces of the fish at a time and sprinkle them with salt and pepper. Fry for 3 to 5 minutes on each side, until they turn golden brown.

6. Transfer the fish to a baking dish. Keep it warm in the oven while you are frying the rest of the fish. Add more oil to the pan as needed.

7. To serve place a large spoonful of rice on each plate, top it with the fish and then cover with the sauce.

Preparation time: 1 hour
Serves 6

Lamb and Rice/ *Skudahkharis*

Somalians often serve this dish to celebrate Eid ul-Fitr or other Islamic festivals.

2 tbsp of vegetable oil

1 onion, chopped

1 clove of garlic, peeled and crushed

450g of boneless lamb,* cut into
    bite-sized pieces

2 tomatoes, chopped

1 tsp of ground cumin

½ tsp of ground cloves

1 tsp of ground cinnamon

2 tbsp of tomato puree

1.2 litres of water

420g of uncooked brown rice

salt and pepper to taste

1. Heat 2 tbsp of oil in a large saucepan over a medium heat. Add the onion, garlic and lamb. Cook for about 5 minutes, or until the meat is browned, stirring constantly.

2. Add the tomatoes, cumin, cloves, cinnamon, tomato puree and water. Stir to combine.

3. Bring the mixture to the boil over a high heat.

4. Add the rice, salt and pepper. Stir.

5. Reduce the heat to low and cover the pan with a tight-fitting lid. Simmer for 30 minutes or until the rice has absorbed all of the water.

6. Remove the pan from the heat and let it stand, covered, for 5 minutes.

7. Serve warm in a large bowl. In Somalia guests eat from the bowl with the fingers of their right hand.

Preparation time: 1 hour
Serves 4

*If lamb is not available or is too expensive, you can use beef or chicken instead.

Lentil Salad / Yamiser Selatta

Ethiopian Christians prepare vegetarian main courses, such as this lentil salad, on days when religious practice forbids them to eat meat.

300g of dried lentils*

1.2 litres of water

1 onion, chopped

2 tbsp of vinegar

6 tbsp of peanut oil or olive oil

3 cloves of garlic, peeled and crushed

½ tsp red chilli flakes

salt and pepper to taste

1. Rinse the lentils in a colander or strainer.

2. In a large saucepan, cover the lentils with 1.2 litres of water and place over a medium heat.

3. Bring to the boil and then lower the heat. Simmer the lentils for 45 minutes or until they are tender, but not mushy.

4. Carefully pour the lentils into a colander to drain.

5. In a medium bowl, combine the onion, vinegar, oil, garlic and chilli flakes.

6. Add the lentils, salt and pepper.

7. Stir and set aside at room temperature for 1 hour. Stir often to blend the flavours.

Preparation time: 2 hours
Serves 6 to 8

*If you are short on time, you can you use tinned lentils and bottled Italian dressing.

East African Plantain Soup/ Supa ya Ndizi

This soup is served in Tanzania for Eid ul-Fitr.

2 or 3 green plantains, peeled

1.4 litres of chicken stock*

salt and pepper to taste

1. Slice the peeled plantains and place them into a food processor.

2. Add 250ml of the stock** and blend until the mixture is smooth.

3. Pour the mixture into a large saucepan. Add the remaining stock.

4. Stir to combine. Cover with a tight-fitting lid and cook over a medium heat for 45 minutes, stirring occasionally.

5. Add salt and pepper to taste.

Preparation time: 1 hour
Serves 4 to 6

* To make the stock place 3 chicken stock cubes into a jug and add 1.4 litres of boiling water. Stir rapidly until the stock cubes have dissolved completely.

** To make this a vegetarian dish use vegetable stock instead of chicken stock.

Index

meat curry 53
menu, East African 28-29

pancakes, rice 33
papaya 40
peanut sauce 45, 48
peanuts: peanut sauce 45, 48;
    kashata 61
pilau 7, 57
plantains 10, 27, 45; boiled 42;
    East African plantain soup 69; fried
    43; grilled 43;

raisins, vermicelli and 42
rice: with fish 65; lamb and 66;
    pancakes 31, 33; *pilau* 7, 57

safety tips 20
salad: avocado and papaya 40; lentil 68
samosas 7, 10, 19, 36-37
sauce 45; *choroku* 46; peanut 45, 48
snacks and appetizers 10, 31; meat on
    a stick 34; *samosas* 7, 10, 19, 36-37
Somalia 7, 13, 66
soup 28, 45; East African plantain 69
spring greens 41
staples 31; *chapatis* 7, 10, 27, 28, 31,
    32, 45; Ethiopian flat bread 17,
    63, 64; rice pancakes 31, 33
stews 10, 17, 28, 45; banana and
    meat 49

Tanzania 7, 8-9, 11, 14, 69

Uganda 7, 9, 17

vegetables 7, 10; casserole 56; *pilau*
    57. *See also* fruits and vegetables
vermicelli and raisins 42
Victoria, Lake 7, 8-9

About the Authors

Bertha Vining Montgomery grew up in Social Circle, Georgia, in the USA. She graduated from Spelman College in Georgia with a degree in home economics. Montgomery has taught in all areas of home economics at high school level. She would like to thank Janet Clemetson, Farha Ibrahim, the Lawal family, Rukiya Mahmood and Uche Iheagwara for their help and encouragement with this book.

Constance Nabwire was born and raised in Uganda. She attended King's College Budo in Uganda before going to the USA on the African Student Program for American Universities. After earning a degree in sociology and psychology from Spelman College in Georgia, Nabwire attended the University of Minnesota on a fellowship by the American Association of University Women and graduated with a masters degree in social work. Nabwire has also published several short stories and articles about her native land. Nabwire would like to thank her friends, who contributed their ideas and recipes to this book.

Photo Acknowledgements
The photographs in this book are reproduced with the permission of: © Joe McDonald/Visuals Unlimited, Inc., pp 2-3; © Robert L. and Diane Wolfe, p 4 (both), 5 (left), 6, 26, 30, 35, 44, 47, 50, 55; © Walter and Louiseann Pietrowicz/September 8th Stock, pp 5 (right), 18, 38, 58, 62, 67; © American Lutheran Church. Used by permission of Augsburg Fortress, pp 11, 15; © Glenn M Oliver/Visuals Unlimited, Inc., p 12; © Phil Porter, p 16; © iStockphoto.com/Frank van den Bergh, p 25.

Cover photos: © Robert L and Diane Wolfe, front (top); © Walter and Louiseann Pietrowicz/September 8th Stock, front (bottom), spine, back.

The illustrations on pages 7, 8, 19, 27, 31, 37, 39, 41, 42, 45, 48, 51, 52, 57, 59, 60, 63, 66, 68, 69 are by Tim Seeley.